THE BOY WHO SAVED HIS FAMILY

GENESIS 37–50 FOR CHILDREN

Written by Alyce Bergey
Illustrated by Betty Wind

Concordia Publishing House

ARCH Books

© 1966 CONCORDIA PUBLISHING HOUSE, ST. LOUIS, MISSOURI
CONCORDIA PUBLISHING HOUSE LTD., LONDON, E. C. 1
MANUFACTURED IN THE UNITED STATES OF AMERICA
ALL RIGHTS RESERVED

Once there was a boy named Joseph.
He was one of thirteen children.
Their father was Jacob.
Their family had lived in the land of Canaan
ever since their great-grandfather Abraham.

Jacob owned many animals.
His children took care of the sheep and goats.

Jacob loved Joseph best of all his sons.
He gave him a long coat with long sleeves;
this showed that Joseph was to be the leader.
The boy was very proud of his coat.

His brothers could see that their father
loved Joseph more than any of them.
They hated Joseph because of this.

Once Joseph told his brothers:
"I dreamed we were tying
bundles of wheat.
Your bundles bowed down to mine.'
This made the brothers angry.

Another time Joseph told them,
"I dreamed that the sun and moon
and eleven stars bowed down to me."
"Do you think we will bow down
to you?" the brothers laughed.

One day Joseph was looking for his brothers.
"Let's kill the dreamer," they said
when they saw him coming.
"No," said the oldest brother.
"Let's put him in this deep hole."

So they took away
his new coat
and put
him in
the deep
hole.

Just then some men rode by.
"Would you like to buy a boy?"
the brothers called out.
"You could sell him in Egypt."
"Yes, we will buy him," said the men.

The brothers put goat's blood
on Joseph's coat.
When Jacob saw the coat, he cried,
"A wild beast has killed my boy."
He was very sad.

On his way to
Egypt Joseph cried,
"Will I ever see Father again?
Why did my brothers do this to me?"

Then Joseph thought:
"God can make bad things
turn out good." Joseph wasn't so
afraid anymore.

In Egypt Joseph was
sold to a rich man.
He had to work without pay.
But his master liked his work,
and God was with him.

One night the king of Egypt
sent for all his wise men.
He said: "I dreamed that I saw
seven fat cows and seven thin cows.
The thin cows ate up the fat ones.

"Then I saw seven good ears of wheat
and seven bad ears of wheat.
The bad ears ate up the good ones.
What does this mean?"
But none of the wise men knew.

Then one of his servants said,
"Joseph knows the meaning of dreams."
The king sent for him at once.
Joseph was a grown man now.

Joseph explained the dreams:
"O king, for seven years
much food will grow,
and for seven years nothing will.
Store up food in the good years.
Then there will be food
for the bad years."

"You are very wise,"
the king told Joseph.
"Take care of things
for me."

The king gave Joseph
new clothes,
and the king's ring
and carriage.

Soon the seven good years came.
Everything grew so that Joseph
had to have new barns built
to store the wheat.

Then came the bad years.
But people could buy food
from Joseph.

So Joseph's big brothers came, too.
They bowed way down before him.
They did not know he was Joseph.
But he knew them.

"You are spies!" he said.
"Oh, no, sir!" they cried.
"We have come only to buy food
for our family."

"No, you are spies," Joseph said.
"Put them in jail!" he ordered.

After three days the brothers
were taken back to Joseph.
"Now we are paying for what we did
to Joseph," they whispered, afraid.

Joseph heard
what they said.
He felt sorry
for them.

"I am Joseph, your brother!" he cried.
"I am not angry with you anymore.
God brought me to Egypt
to save us all from hunger."

The brothers
were so happy!
They had long
been sorry for
what they had
done to Joseph.

They went to get
the whole family.

How happy Jacob was!
"Lord," he cried, "You are taking
such good care of us."

God said: "I shall go with you to Egypt.
Someday I will bring your family back
and give them this land."

Jacob and his children moved to Egypt.
Joseph cried for joy when he saw his father.

The family got sacks of flour,
and good grass land for their animals.
And God was with them.
But one day they would return home.

Dear Parents:

The story of Joseph is not just an adventure tale, standing all by itself. It is a story about how God can change even the worst things into something good and wonderful in His own good time. It forms a part of the great adventure of the people of God, Israel, and of God's saving plan for mankind.

God had brought Joseph's great-grandfather Abraham into the land of Canaan, there to bring up a new people who would differ from all the surrounding nations by their faith in Him. Nothing could block God's saving plan; not even such disasters as famine or the actions of Abraham's great-grandchildren could. Sold into slavery by his brothers, Joseph became God's instrument in the saving of Egypt and his own people from hunger. The family tragedy became their salvation, and eventually ours because it was from Abraham's family that the Saviour of all nations was to be born.

Can you help your child see the deeper meaning of the Joseph story and recall it in times of fear and anxiety? And will you help him grow not only in knowing the various Bible stories but also in understanding how they belong to one great plan of God?

THE EDITOR